the Cat

A guide to selection, care, nutrition,

behaviour, health, breeding and play.

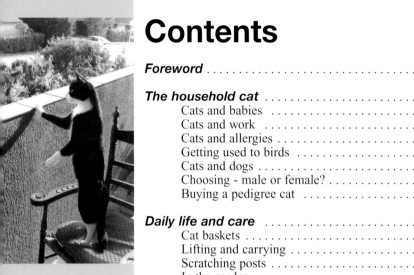

Contents

Foreword

Taking on a cat is something special. The impending arrival of a new family member is something to look forward to but it can also raise some questions. Especially if it's your very first cat. Will it feel at home with you? What does it need to eat, how does it stay fit? Can you take it with you on holiday and what do you do if it disappears?

This book is written to help you on your way to an enjoyable relationship with your cat. The cat should enjoy being in your home but it's equally important that you are able to relax and enjoy your experiences with your cat. The chapters that follow cover a number of important subjects and offer practical tips and professional advice to help get to know your cat.

A number of the subjects may not be of immediate interest but they will be useful for reference in the future. Here and there references are made to other titles in the About Pets series that go into particular topics in more depth than is possible in this guide.

About Pets

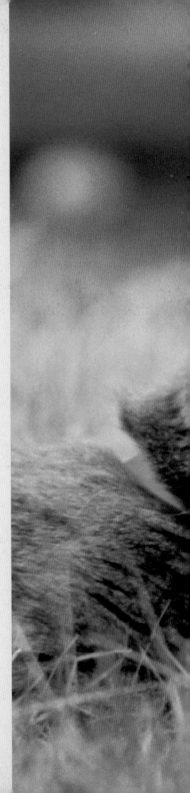

A Publication of About Pets.

Copyright © 2003
About Pets
co-publisher United Kingdom
Kingdom Books
PO9 5TL, England

ISBN 1852792191
First printing
September 2003

Original title: *de Praktische kattenwijzer*
© 2000 - 2003 Welzo Media Productions bv,
About Pets,
Warffum, the Netherlands
http://www.aboutpets.org

Photos:
Welzo Media Productions,
Anneke Tasseron, Isabelle Francios
Rob Dekker and readers of
the About Pets magazine

Printed in Italy

The household cat

Maybe you already have a cat. Perhaps you would love to have a cat but for personal reasons you're not sure if it's a wise decision. This chapter covers a few of the most frequently asked questions about buying a cat.

Cats and babies

One of the most asked questions is: Can we have a cat now that we have a baby? In principle there is nothing against it, cats are house-trained, clean animals and research has shown that keeping one or more pets can be beneficial for a young child's development

Cats enjoy lying in warm, comfortable spots and there is no cosier place than a child's cot, which is where the baby is mostly. If you don't want your cat to share the baby's cot all you need to do is to ensure that the cat can't get into the baby's room. You can also remove the cat from the bed each time it climbs in and place it in its own basket. If you say 'No!' and give it a stroke as you put it in its own basket the cat will quickly

learn that it's not allowed to jump into the baby's cot.

In principle little can happen even if the cat and your baby do take a nap together. A cat is a very sensitive animal and it will move immediately it feels any pressure on its body. You naturally need to keep an eye on things though: a cornered cat will use its nails to escape so there is always a risk of scratching! It's of course not wise to let an 11 pound (5 kilogram) male cat sleep with a new-born baby.

Cats and work

If you work away from home it's never a bad thing for your cat to have the company of another cat. Cats are happier with company but if needs be they don't mind being on their own. Even cats can get bored though and if this is the case they will start playing pranks. This happens quicker with a relatively young cat than with a mature cat. If you only have one cat at home don't be surprised if the houseplants are uprooted, the washing basket is emptied and the content dragged through the house, or that crystal flower vase is smashed to smithereens during your absence. If your cat would have had a playmate the ideas might never have come into its head. The best playmate is a cat of the same age but a slightly older cat can also be good company.

If you have to be away from home all day, take a couple of precautions to make your absence as pleasant as possible. A cat always needs to be able to drink. Make sure that enough drinking water is always available and don't forget to take the weather into account. If it's warm cats drink more than normal. Make your house as safe as possible. Don't leave windows ajar because cats only need a very small opening to escape. If you don't leave your cat any food during the day you can be sure of receiving a royal welcome when you get back!

Cats and allergies

Many people are allergic to particular allergens and yet still keep a cat as a pet. Remarkably this group includes people who are also allergic to cats albeit slightly allergic.

If you are allergic, but would still like to keep a cat, it's sensible to discuss it with your doctor first. It may be that he or she will advise you against it for health reasons but as long as it's not explicitly discouraged you are free to try. Keep in mind though that it could end up in disappointment. If it does turn out that you are allergic then the cat will have to go, and if you have already become attached to the animal the parting could an unpleasant experience for both of you.

The problem with allergies lies in the fact that it's difficult to predict in advance whether and how your allergy will bother you.

Only experience will tell. Anybody who gives away or sells a cat will be able to understand that somebody with an allergy will first want to see if they can share their daily life with the cat, and only then decide if they want to keep it or not. As a buyer however, you need to take into account that not everybody will be happy to accept a fourteen day trial period with the possibility of getting the animal back from you if it's not suitable.

Getting used to birds

In the wild cats live on small rodents and birds. Birds awaken the cat's hunting instinct, even indoors. Small birds mostly feel unprotected and unsafe in the presence of a cat. If a cat gets especially close, birds can take flight and wound or even kill themselves by flying into the walls of their cage or aviary.

It's not only in the wild that cats can exercise great patience waiting to get a bite to eat, it happens

indoors as well. When a cat and a canary or parakeet are living together the cat sometime spends a lot of time working out how to get into the cage despite the barriers. Strangely enough many people are amazed when the cat finally finds a way to reach the cage, opens the door and release the bird, only to hunt and finally eat it. Even if cats and birds are both pets, one will always want to feed on the other and will instinctively continue to do so. That's' why it's best to choose a cat or a bird but not both.

Cats and dogs

The idea that cats and dogs are each other's arch-enemies was consigned to history long ago. Cats and dogs live peacefully with each other in many families without a problem. Despite this it's not true that any cat or any dog will accept each other. Cats and dogs that have grown up in each other's company will be able to share a lifelong friendship because they have become adapted to each other and feel themselves to be full members of their family. Superficial differences of opinion occur now and again of course but real arguments seldom surface.

There is little to stop you taking a young cat and a young dog into your home at the same time but unless they have had earlier contact with a dog or a cat you will have to allow them enough time to get used to each other. Young animals are very playful, so their play in any case will give them the opportunity to get to know each other and learn how to live with each other.

British Shorthair

Siamese

Maine Coon

Abessinian

It will be more difficult to get an older cat and a dog used to each other, especially if the dog is also mature and perhaps has had less than enjoyable experiences with cats in the past. In this case it's important that you consciously give the animal that's been with you the longest the feeling that you still care. The newcomer will demand much of your attention so if you want to avoid jealousies developing you will need to divide your attention equally.

Choosing - female or male?

If you choose a male you will never be tempted to breed a litter of kittens. Should you think that you might want to do this at some time then you should naturally choose a female.

If you chose a male it's best to have him castrated (assuming it's not already been done by the previous owner). Castration will prevent the male from spraying urine and reduce his tendency to fight other males. He will also be unable to father young from any chance encounters he may have if he is allowed outside. Males in general have a slightly softer character than females, who can often be a little domineering. A male will for example accept another cat or dog as a family member quite easily and they can be very affectionate and playful.

Young females, like young males, are playful animals. Once mature

they regularly come into heat and start to display rather moody behaviour. In any event adult females are less uninhibited and spontaneous than (castrated or un-castrated) males. Every animal has its individual character of course so don't allow the sex to be the deciding factor should you fall for a particular cat. You're sure to be able to get on well with him or her!

Buying a pedigree cat

If you decide to buy a pedigree cat it's very important to find yourself

a reliable breeder. Every cat society has a kitten agency. This means that they maintain lists of kittens offered for sale by breeders.

As soon as you know the breed of the kitten you want to buy you should check with the relevant kitten agency to see if there is a breeder in the area with kittens available. If so then you can have yourself placed on a waiting list to be contacted as soon as a litter is born. Some breeds are rare; others are seldom bred, so you may need to be patient.

Never buy a pedigree cat from just anybody at a Sunday market or from a commercial breeder. In most cases these cats are have not been checked for inherited disorders and they will be poorly socialised. The majority of breeders are members of a breed association, and breed and keep their cats with a true love for the business. They will be happy to support you with advice about how to get on with your cat and help if you should get into difficulties.

Daily life and care

Even if a cat can be considered a relatively 'easy animal', it still demands time and energy. In addition to requiring daily care it also has to learn what it may and may not do within the family.

A well kept cat is less likely to get sick; a cat that obeys the rules of the house is enjoyable company and doesn't create any nuisance.

Cat basket

Cats will always find a cosy place to sleep and your bed will often be its preference! Nevertheless a cat also likes to withdraw to its own basket once in a while.
A wide variety of cat baskets are on sale in pet shops but you need to make sure that the one you buy is big enough for your cat. The cat must be able to stretch out in it in any position it likes. If you have a young cat buy a basket large enough for the cat to grow into.

The classic cat basket is made of reed. All you need to do is add a small blanket or a cushion. Wash these regularly, just like you would anything else that your cat frequently comes into contact with. From the standpoint of hygiene, reed baskets are not very practical: should your cat vomit they are not at all easy to clean. There are also plastic and foam rubber baskets. The plastic ones are very easy to clean and disinfect should it be necessary. A small blanket or cushion is also needed for this type of basket. Foam rubber baskets are finished with a material cover that can sometimes be unzipped for washing. In an emergency the foam rubber basket can be put into the washing machine complete.

Lifting and carrying

Some people mistakenly believe that a cat should be picked up by the scruff of the neck. Only the mother may pickup a kitten by the scruff of its neck and even she will only do it if it's really necessary, for example to bring it to safety. If you were to pick up your cat by the scruff of its neck you would cause it pain, especially if the cat is a little on the heavy side. The reflex of cats picked up in this way is to hang completely limp. You should only hold a cat by the scruff of its neck in exceptional circumstances, for example if you need to give it a pill and the cat is difficult to control. The vet will also hold your cat by the scruff of the neck while it's being vaccinated.

The only correct way to pick up a cat is to support it with one hand under the breast, directly behind the front legs. As you lift it up support its rear legs with your free hand carrying it upright to lie against your chest. Children are especially fond of picking cats up and dragging them around but they are often a little hard handed. Teach children how a cat should be picked up and carried. Show them how it's done and explain to them that a cat feels cornered if held too tightly and will use its nails and maybe even its teeth to free itself. Never lift a cat only by its front legs! Even a young cat is too heavy to be lifted this way. Picking up a cat the wrong way can result in physical injury.

Scratching posts

Scratching is a natural necessity for a cat. They do this not only to

Your pet shop has a wide choice in scratching posts and other cat supplies

sharpen their nails but also to mark their territory. On top of that they simply like to get their nails stuck into something and enjoy a good stretch. In the wild this behaviour causes no nuisance at all, but indoors the wallpaper or furniture generally suffer. You can avoid damage to your interior simply by buying a scratching post. These are available in all shapes and sizes at pet shops. A good scratching post must be stable so that it can't fall over. The cat must be able to stand stretched upright against it, and it must be covered with rough material (carpet for example) that has a vertical texture. Place the post in a part of the house the cat loves to visit. Adding a couple of drops of catnip will make it even more attractive. Cats are crazy about the smell of catnip.

In the garden

Cats regard birds as prey. Birds flying overhead attract attention even though the cat knows that they are out of reach. Birds are not however the only prey and cats are also attracted to rabbits, mice and hedgehogs. Anybody who lets a cat into the garden shouldn't be surprised or annoyed to be presented with a dead bird.

Many cats are well fed at home and capture prey instinctively without the intention of eating them.

Healthy adult birds are generally able to escape stalking cats. Young birds just able to fly and scratching around on the ground devote all their attention to parents arriving with food. They are not used to keeping an eye out for enemies and are easy prey for an opportunistic cat.

If you want to let your cat into the garden now and again, do your best to prevent it from getting at birds nests. A collar with a bell attached will usually give birds enough warning but it's best to keep your cat inside in the spring and the beginning of the summer when young birds are leaving their nests.

Getting used to other cats

It's not difficult to get two young cats used to each other. In fact they do it themselves by playing, sleeping and eating from the same bowl together. It's exceptional for two young cats not to accept each other and it actually only occurs with cats that are born and raised in total isolation.

The majority of cats that have had their own place in a household for several years are not too happy about the arrival of another cat. For an older cat it's unpleasant and alien to have to allow a stranger into its territory because, apart

from the territory, the cats very existence is threatened. There will be 'arguments' at the very least of course that produce hissing, growling and paw fights. Shut the older cat up in one of the rooms to make sure that the new cat has the opportunity to explore the house in peace. Once the new cat has had time to get to know the building, including where the litter box, feeding bowls and drinking bowls are located, let both cats into the living room under supervision. Leave the room door open so that both cats have an escape route available to them should a fight develop. Don't make an old cat jealous by devoting all your time to the new cat. Understand that the oldest cat also has 'grandfather' rights! Don't force anything while they are getting to know each other. It can sometimes take a little time but they should be used to each other within a week or two.

Timid cats

Some cats will make friends with anybody, sit on any lap and let everybody stroke them. Other cats have a definite preference for calm and softly spoken people, often those who are not particularly fond of cats and whose behaviour is adjusted so as to be as inconspicuous to the cat as possible. This behaviour often has the opposite and undesirable effect of attracting the cat to sit on the persons lap. Other cats show a clear preference either for men or for women.

Timid cats like the person they become attached to a lot but have no time at all for strangers. The physical signs are running away when visitors arrive, or hissing or growling if approached by a stranger. Some cats are so timid that they even dive under a cupboard at the first ring of the doorbell.

A young cat that behaves this way can still be re-socialised but it's more difficult with older cats. It depends on how the cat's behaviour came about in the first place and how long it's been going on for. Never restrain a cat against its will. Try to keep it in the room when people visit, but don't force it to stay there. Talk calmly with visitors and don't make any unexpected movements. Let your cat get gradually used to as many men, women and children as possible. Pay absolutely no attention to the cat if it growls and certainly don't reward the behaviour by stroking it or comforting it.

Baths

Cats are clean animals and they wash themselves regularly. Their tongues are covered by horny papilla, you might have felt when a cat licked you. Its tongue feels like a piece of rough sandpaper.

In the wild the rough tongue helps members of the cat family to lick fleshy remains from the bones of their prey; domestic cats use the roughness to keep their fur clean.

Cat breeders often bath their long haired cats a couple of days before an exhibition to make its coat as full and soft as possible. Unless a cat has a skin disorder and a vet prescribes a medicinal bath it doesn't actually need a bath. It's unnecessary and undesirable to bath a cat (too often). Its coat is naturally shiny and resilient and protects the skin and the body. Cats remove the majority of dust and loose hair from their coats with their tongues. You can remove any remains by combing and brushing. If a cat's coat is washed too often the natural fat layer will disappear and it will get dirty quicker and quicker.

If it should be necessary to bath your cat, the following is important: Use a special cat shampoo and tepid water (maximum 104°F/40 °C); rinse well so that no shampoo at all remains. Towel the cat dry and use a hairdryer (not on the highest setting!). Don't use a showerhead because cats can be frightened by the noise these can make. Use just the hose. Only let the cat out once it's completely dry.

Grooming

How frequently you need to comb and brush your cat will depend on the hair. There are cats with normal short hair and cats with long hair such as Persians. Longhaired cats are more prone to problems because the coat structure is thinner and softer and it gets easily tangled with old dead hairs that are difficult to remove. That's why longhaired cats need to be combed and brushed every other day.

Shorthaired cats are much less demanding but even they need to be brushed occasionally. Every other week is sufficient but a little more often during the moulting season. During moulting they lose more hair than normal and you will notice it because you will find lots of loose hair around the house.
Cats with long hair, but a coat that's not as thick as the hair of a Persian, can be brushed every four days.

Use the correct material: combs must not be sharp or they will damage the cat's skin. Choose a natural hair or rubber brush. Comb the hair thoroughly being careful not to damage the skin. You should always try to untangle knotted hair with your fingers first. If you're unsuccessful cut the knots free with a pair of scissors. Always comb from head to tail. Once the coat is free of knots give the cat a good final brush. A healthy coat should be shiny regardless of its

colour. Pay special attention to the fur on the belly and between the legs where knots most often occur.

Cat litter

There are a number of ways of filling a cat litter box. Peat dust was used in the past but it wasn't very good at absorbing the odours of urine and droppings. An alternative is newspaper. Even though it's suitable and cheap it's practically impossible to maintain a supply large enough for a household with two or more cats. Some people use sand. Cats love to dig into sand to do the necessary but sand or earth always have to be collected from somewhere and they are relatively heavy. Cleaning cat litter is not exactly an enjoyable experience and a filling of sand or earth doesn't make it any more pleasant. Sawdust and wood shavings have the same disadvantage as peat dust: they don't absorb the unpleasant smells very well, and the material is so lightweight that it often sticks to the cats legs and gets walked around outside the cat litter box.

All things considered, cat grit works best. You can buy it in quantities sufficient for a week or bulk sizes suitable for a couple of months. Litter generates dust when is poured into the litter box so be sure not to inhale it. Spread a thin layer in the litter box and remove the cat's droppings as frequently as possible. You can dispose of them in the toilet as long as they are litter free. Different sorts of litter are available from rough to fine granules so you will need to find out with practice which sort you and your cat prefer.

Hazards in and around the home

Unsuitable toys such as easily swallowed foam rubber balls or marbles are a serious danger for a cat. String can also be hazard if a cat gets tangled up in it. Sharp objects such as scissors, needles, pins, drawing pins, nails and glass can inflict injury. Don't allow your cat into the kitchen while you are cooking. Hot gas rings, electric hotplates and pans of boiling water are a real risk too. Check the washing machine before you use it. As surprising as it may seem, cats like to hid in them and quite a few cats have already drowned in them!

Another favourite place is a warm tumble drier. Screen off your balcony if your cat is allowed access. Block the entrance to ledges along roof guttering. Cats are super inquisitive and think that they can walk along even the narrowest edges. Keep cleaning materials (washing up liquid, bleach and toilet cleaner), painting materials (paint thinners, turpentine, chemicals), insecticides and medicines out of your cat's reach. Dangers lurk in other items as well, such as electrical wiring (can be bitten through!), hot irons, lit candles and toxic houseplants. Outdoors cats run the risks of traffic, weed killers and rat poisons, poisonous garden plants and, in extreme cases, cat haters. Fence off your garden and keep your cat safe.

Toys

Cats are not only playful as kittens; much older cats like to play too. Playing keeps a cat physically and mentally fit so it's good to take a little time every day to play with your cat. All sorts of cat toys are available from pet shops. Many cats are happy with simple things like a crackly ball of paper. The pleasure seems to be never ending with them slapping it into the air, running after it and bringing it back to you in their mouth. Household objects can have the same effect. Very playful young cats don't even need toys. They jump up and down trying to catch dust hanging in sunlit air. Some cats find the belt of a dressing gown an irresistible attraction. They can play with it endlessly, as if it's a snake, jumping on it, biting it, throwing it into the air and then dragging it to a safe place.

Balls are especially popular but they should be too big to swallow. Ping-Pong balls are the most suitable.
Most cats love pieces of string but make sure that they don't get tangled up in them. Elastic is unsuitable because it can be eaten and cause suffocation.

In the car and walking

Never let your cat travel in a car unrestrained. If something unexpected were to happen they could panic and get trapped under your feet or under the accelerator or brake pedals. The consequences don't bear thinking about. Even if you're going somewhere by foot you should never simply hold your cat in your arms or on your shoulder.

Even if your cat is relaxed and self-assured something unexpected can always happen which could frighten it and it will escape faster than you can think. Special cat harnesses are available that attach to their collars. These harnesses are handy for travelling on public transport or by car. They leave your cat free to move about but you can still restrain it if it tries to make a run for it. Never use a harness to walk your cat because dogs, children appearing out of nowhere, screeching tyres or a vehicle horn can frighten them into climbing up you with their nails extended.

The best way to transport your cat is in a travel basket. A range of models is available from pet shops. The cat will feel safe and it won't be able to escape.

Outside day and night

It's a fact that cats like to be outdoors. They can lie in the sun, breathe in fresh air, forage around in the grass and between bushes, listen for the sounds of birds and other animals, in short: out of doors the cat is in its natural environment. This doesn't mean that cats aren't

content inside, they can be as long as they are kept busy and don't end up leading an existence lacking any stimulation.

Your cat is best off in the garden but that doesn't mean that is a good idea to leave it in the garden day and night. That's the quickest way to turn a cat into a tramp. Once a cat has lost its bond with its home and family, it will leave. As long as you make sure to stick to precise feeding times every day as far as practically possible, your cat will always come back to eat.

Anybody leaving a cat outside should be aware of the risks. Cats can become victims of traffic accidents, poisoning by accident or design. Un-castrated males can have bloody fights with other males and inconveniently father offspring with un-sterilised females who can become pregnant several times a year.

It's preferable to keep your cat indoors whenever the weather is bad and at night-time. This way it gets the freedom it needs while remaining attached to you and the creature comforts of your home.

Food

Cats are very choosy eaters. They have a very sensitive digestive system so it's in your cats best interest that it be given a well thought out diet: a balanced menu that will keep your cat healthy.

Meals

Just how often a cat needs to eat depends primarily on its age. Young cats need enough energy to develop their bodies, which is why they need to be feed more often each day than adult cats. Adult cats can manage on two meals a day from about eighteen months onwards. If they get dried cat food and snacks in addition to the regular meals then one meal per day is enough. A cat recovering from illness needs several meals a day. Highly nutritional protein rich food is especially suitable for young cats. A cat is fully mature from about eight years old when its feeding requirements change again. There is a special diet for older and geriatric cats but no matter how old your cat is: it needs a constant supply of fresh drinking water!

Strange preferences

Some cats display rather strange taste preferences. As long as it doesn't get too strange it's best to accept it but bear in mind that it might indicate that the cat is suffering from a shortage of something in particular. For example eating a lot of high salt foods may indicate a salt shortage.

Cats are highly specialised protein eaters and their digestive systems are specially adapted for it. The intestines are short which means that they can't obtain all the nutrients they need only from potatoes and gravy. Starch must be easily digestible if cats are to be able to extract the carbohydrates they need. This is a remnant of life in the wild: the grain that its wild forefathers consumed was

already part digested in the intestines of their prey.

Don't give your cat any strongly spiced or salted food: its kidneys are very sensitive and adapted to process   digestible proteins. A cat should preferably not eat simply what everybody else is eating. It's best not to give it pieces of sausage or fish because they are often too salty, smoked or spicy. If you want to spoil your cat a variety of cat snacks are available from pet shops.

Cats like milk but can't digest the lactose it contains very well and it often results in diarrhoea. As an alternative you can best give your cat special cat milk in which the lactose content has been adjusted. Most cats don't like the taste of sweet things unless they are mixed with fat, such as whipping cream. It's true that sweet things and fruit are not in themselves bad for a cat but you need to give them in moderation or their digestive system will become unbalanced.

Eating together

A couple of cats that get on well with each other can eat out of the same bowl. Some people with a number of cats even give food in one large bowl without any problem at all.

Sometimes, eating together has a positive effect on cats: they start eating once they see other cats

eating. Having another cat to set the pace and stimulate the others can be a good thing, for example if you have a sick cat that needs to eat well to help it recover. But there are cases when individual bowls may be better.

Some cats become so excited by eating in a group that they eat progressively faster and faster. Apart from simply eating too fast it, means that some of the cats won't get enough. If you give your cats separate bowls it will be easier to keep a check on how much each is eating, and if a cat needs to go on a diet it will in any event need an adjusted portion in its own bowl. Even if you have a separate bowl for each of your cats, where you physically put them is just as important. If bowls are too close to each other it has the same effect as if you were using one bowl. Put cat A therefore in one corner of the kitchen and cat B in the opposite corner.

When you open a can of cat food both cats will get used to going to their own corner without prompting.

Choosy eaters

Cats are often difficult eaters but there might be a physical reason of course, such as dental problems. Always consult your vet if you're in doubt about your cat's health. Even healthy cats can sometimes be difficult eaters eating too little; very irregularly, or suddenly rejecting something they always loved.

A fickle eating pattern is often the result of how a cat was raised. Cat's that were only given fish to eat in the early days of their lives, for example, may have difficulty as they get older with menus that vary. It's the breeder's responsibility to give kittens a varied diet as soon as they go onto regular food to avoid the problem.

Yawn!!

It's also important to work to a fixed meal schedule. Cats are habitual animals and feel at their best when they eat, rest, play and sleep at specific times. Once a daily pattern is established you will notice that your cat will come and ask to be fed should you be too late for one reason or another. Give your cat about 30 minutes or so to eat the food you put in front of it, then remove it. This way the cat will learn in time that it has to eat when it's given food. Limit extras and in-between meals to rewards during training, for example when you're teaching it to use the scratching post. Don't give it food direct from the refrigerator or from the cooker. Allow the food time to reach room temperature first. Food that's too hot or too cold can upset your cat's digestive system.

Canned and other foods

Canned and other ready-to-serve food is generally good quality. It might seem attractive to give a cat fresh food but it's not quite that simple in practice, certainly if you want to give it a complete diet. It's difficult for the inexperienced to find the right balance between proteins, fats and carbohydrates. The correct amounts of vitamins, minerals and trace elements are impossible to judge. Apart from giving too little vitamins, there are a large number of vitamins of which you can give too much.

In both cases the consequences for cats can be disastrous. Maintaining the calcium level of a carnivore (the cat is a flesh eater) is a compli-cated task on its own. The phospho-rous content of its food must be in the correct proportion to the calci-um content; if it's not, the cat's health will suffer (osteoporosis). You are better off using good quali-ty ready-to-serve food to prevent this sort of problem from arising. These products are balanced and provide a cat with everything it needs.

Supplements such as vitamin pre-parations are unnecessary and can be damaging! Eating fresh raw meat introduces other risks. The cat can become infected with Toxoplasma, a parasite that can also be passed to humans, which can have serious consequences for a foetus or very young children.

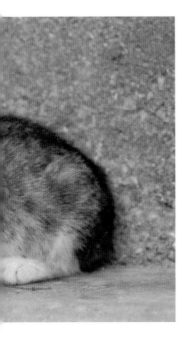

fur balls from its stomach. Cats swallow fur while they are grooming themselves but are unable to digest it. Green food is a natural stimulant that helps the cat to vomit.

Cats are crazy about grazing on particular houseplants. Especially papyrus and other sap rich, grass type plants. You can prevent this if you provide a tray of special cat grass. This is fast growing soft oat grass can be bought in pet shops and garden centres or at markets. The majority of cats like it and eat it regularly. You will certainly come across a little vomit from time to time but it's very important that your cat is able to get rid of its fur balls and cat grass is an essential part of your cat care supplies.

Meat must always be cooked before it's given. Cats can also contract Aujeszky's disease by eating raw or inadequately cooked pork. This disease is resistant to medicines and results in death.

Plants

Sooner or later every cat owner will see his or her cat trying to eat house or garden plants. Whatever you do, you need to discourage it because some plants are toxic. With a little luck damage will be limited to digestion problems but the results can be deadly, so you need to make sure that your houseplants don't present any danger. A cat doesn't eat plants without good reason and in most cases it's looking for green food to help it expel

If your cat still insists on eating houseplants, you can also try to discourage it by saying 'naughty' in a reprimanding tone and by trying to distract its attention. Lead the cat to the cat grass or play with it. If this doesn't help, you can try spraying the cat with a plant spray just as long as you make sure the cat isn't aware that you are the one that's doing the spraying. You must always discipline your cat the moment it attacks a plant. Doing it after the event won't have the desired effect because the cat won't understand why you are doing it.

A summary of toxic house and garden plants can be found on page 59.

Breeding

Reproduction is an important aspect of a cat's instinctive behaviour. People who simply want company will probably be as happy to miss the recurring joys of virile males and female cats in heat as they would tooth ache.

Nevertheless it's still good to know a little about cat breeding so that you can take the steps necessary, should you so wish, to prevent kittens.

In heat

Females regularly become fertile or, come into heat. Changes in their behaviour and the way they smell indicate that they are ready and willing to mate. The odour is detectable to male cats but not to man. Because cats don't have a very sensitive sense of smell females in heat use their voices to attract males.

Coming in heat begins with the female becoming more affectionate. She rubs her head and back against tables, chairs and human legs often meowing more fre-

quently and with a rougher sounding voice than normal. As the process progresses the signs become more evident. Some females, especially Siamese and related cats, will occasionally urinate indoors to establish a so-called territorial flag. At a particular moment the cat will lie relaxed on the ground and start rolling on her axis. She pauses repeatedly to wash away a light vaginal discharge.

At the peak of the process the female pulls a typical in heat face: the whisker pads swell up spreading the whiskers forwards. She doesn't walk normally but crouches. If she is touched she turns her tail away from the vagina and raises her hindquarters treading rhythmically against the floor with her hind legs. This is the right moment for intercourse to take place.

As far as behaviour is concerned, females in heat are more affectionate than normal. She would never allow a male to have intercourse with her without this behavioural change. The season lasts for about nine days and reoccurs two or three times a year, but in some cats, such as Siamese, more often.

Prevention

The surest method to prevent cats from coming into heat is by spaying. In this case, temporary signs such as loud meowing and incontinence belong well and truly to the past, and there will be no risk of your cat suddenly surprising you with a new litter of kittens.

If you're considering producing litters at some time in the future you can make a female temporarily infertile by using the pill. Generally the contraceptive pill for cats is effective in suppressing the signs of being in-heat, but every now and again a cat might still show the signs. This is mostly however due to incorrect dosage being used or the cat having spat out the pill unnoticed. Unfortunately, it's often already too late and the female will have already become pregnant. There is also an contraceptive injection for females. The vet can prevent the

signs developing for periods of between three and six months. The majority of females are still infertile when they first come into heat following use of the conception pill or injection, so skip the first one if you want to produce a litter.

When you are sure that you do not want your cat to have any (more) kittens you are better off to have her spayed. The operation also reduces the risk of milk gland tumours that can often be malignant in cats.

The first litter

In principle, a cat can become pregnant the first time she comes into heat. Depending on the breed a cat can come in heat as early as five or six months, regular cats mostly a little later. Because of this you need to be able to recognise the signs and keep your cat inside in good time.

When you take on a young male and young female at the same time, you need to stay alert. Some cats can become pregnant at a very young age. It doesn't happen that often, but the risks are real. Get your vet involved in good time to do something about family planning.

If you want a litter of kittens it's best to wait until your female is about a year old and has had time to mature physically and mentally.

Mating

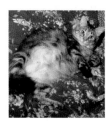

Pregnant cat

Check in advance that good homes are available for the kittens. If you can't be sure of takers then it's better not to start breeding.

Nursery

Cats prefer to give birth in a peaceful place. A living room is fine as long as it's not too busy. Three weeks before the birth you can put cartons in place lined with a layer of cellular nappies for the cat to make a nest for its young.

Mothers and new kittens need rest but they don't need to be isolated. Kittens need to get used to people and noises quite quickly, otherwise they will remain timid for the rest of their lives.

Warmth is very important for the mother and her children. The temperature in the nursery needs to be about 77 °F (25 °C) because young cats that get cold won't do well and they can even die from hypothermia. If the room is cold, either hang an infrared heat lamp over the nest, use a heat mat or a well wrapped hot water bottle. Use a thermometer regularly to ensure that the temperature remains constant.

Rest if very important. If the mother gets the feeling that it's not peaceful enough she will drag her kittens to a place she thinks is safer. The dragging in itself is not good for the young so make sure that the there is a relaxed atmosphere in the house. The kitten's eyes need to get used to light very gradually so you need to make

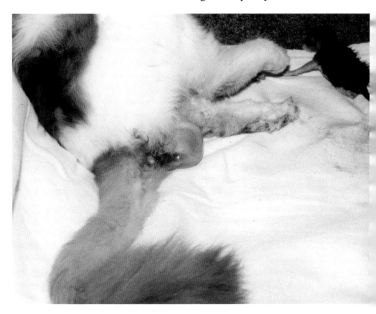

sure that the light in the nursery is not too bright. If necessary, you should close curtains or blinds.

Delivery

Nature normally takes its own course and a female can in principle give birth without human intervention. Of course, that doesn't mean that you can step out to do the shopping if your cat is about to give birth. She might just need your help because of her inexperience in looking after newly born young.

The birth is announced by contractions. When the mother's body contracts, the unborn young can sometimes be seen as bumps under the cat's fur. It can take a while before the first kitten is born, especially if it's a first pregnancy. If nothing has happened after a couple of hours you should call the vet.

On average, four kittens are born per litter (more or less than four is therefore normal). About half an hour elapses between the births of each kitten, which means that the average litter takes about two hours to be born, assuming that there are no complications.

The afterbirth, which follows each kitten as it's born, is eaten by the mother. She also bites through each umbilical cord but these should not be shorter than one inch (2.5 cm). The placentas need

to be removed from the noses of the new-born or they will suffocate. Help the mother as necessary.

A mother licking a kitten dry is enough to stimulate it into to breathing. If she starts to give birth to a new kitten you can carefully towel dry one born earlier. When you're finished, lay it so that it can drink from one of the mother's teats. The mother may be in pain from contractions so you need to make sure that she doesn't lay or lean on the young animal without noticing it. If you're doubtful about anything concerning the birth always contact your vet. Even after an easy birth, have the mother and kittens checked out to be sure they are in good health.

The mother cat eats the afterbirth

Castration, sterilisation and spaying

Castrating a male cat is a simple operation carried out under local anaesthetic, whereby the testes and sperm ducts are removed. As soon as the anaesthetic has worn off, the cat is back to normal. After castration, no more sperm is produced and the male is infertile. Castration in females is called spaying.

Spaying removes the uterus and ovaries. The female can no longer bear young and will no longer go into heat. In sterilisation only the fallopian tubs are tied off. The female can't get pregnant but she

will still go into heat. Before you decide to have your cat spayed, you must be quite sure that you won't want her to bear any (more) litters because the operation is irreversible.

Spaying offers a big advantage, even for a female that's always kept inside; she will never again go into heat. It's also a good solution for owners of outdoor cats that can become very loud when they are in heat attracting all sorts of males from the surrounding area into the garden. Another advantage is that it brings an end to the temporary incontinence that some cats suffer from when they are in-heat. A spayed female often has a more even character. Males should in fact always be castrated, otherwise sooner or later they will be spraying urine all over the place and the odour is unbearable. If a male is castrated in time, the

spraying behaviour mostly never shows itself.

The best age

Males are normally castrated when they are about six months old and have had time to develop a more or less adult posture.

When a young male cat begins displaying adult male behaviour, it's not only because a female is in the area. An un-castrated male will start spraying or spouting urine and cover everything with it - chair legs, the stairs and corners of the room, holding his trembling tail high, sometimes treading the ground with his hind legs. He does this to mark his territory, inside and outside. The moment you notice that this behaviour is about to start you need to get him castrated without delay, because once it has started it's difficult to train then, not to spray. The less he has sprayed before the operation, the greater the chance is that the behaviour will disappear.

You can have a female spayed when she is around 6 months old. It's often said that females should only be spayed after they had had their first litter, and that this is healthier. The fact is that it makes no physical difference if the female is still a virgin when she is spayed. There is no psychological difference either: a female cat does not "miss" having had any young. Not all females are naturally good mothers and in the end the respon-

sibility for finding the kittens a good home is yours alone. If you can't guarantee it, it's better to have you childless female spayed than to allow her to have her first litter.

Castration and laziness

Contrary to popular belief, cats don't become dull or lazy once they have been sterilised, spayed or castrated. Their weight will increase but your vet should be able to suggest a diet that will prevent this, it could be that your cat is getting a little too much to eat in any case. As any tendency to gain weight increases with the change in their hormonal balance, lack of exercise will further increase the probability of them getting fat. Spayed females in general are more playful then they were before their surgery. With their reproductive hormones less of an influence, they have more time and attention to devote to other things. You can indeed play a role in influencing them. Play along whenever you notice that your castrated male or spayed female is hunting something. Throw a crackling ball of paper for them to retrieve. Most cats do this naturally anyway without having to learn it. You can keep your cat active and fit by stimulating it to play.

Behaviour

A little insight into cat behaviour is important if you are going to enjoy living together. It also helps if your cat understands a few 'house rules'. These are easily taught because cats learn easily

Scratching post training

Having taken a cat into your home, you naturally don't want it to scratch the furniture and wallpaper so you will need to teach it to use a scratching post.

Make sure it's ready from the moment the cat arrives.

Immediately you see the cat is about to scratch a place where you don't want it to, bring the cat to the scratching post. Hook its nails in the post's material and see how the cat reacts. If it goes back to the place it had originally chosen then you need to correct it with your voice. A strict 'Naughty!' will be understood but you shouldn't forbid too much during the learning phase, because at the same time you are trying to build a relationship with your cat.

Be consistent and continue to take your cat to the scratching post. This means that in the beginning you will have to keep an eye on what your cat is doing and be one jump ahead anytime it looks like it's going to sink its claws into something you love. Your cat will soon understand what you expect of it. You can speed up the process by sprinkling a few drops of catnip on the post. A cat treat as a reward also works well.

Collars and leads

It's handy to let a cat get used to wearing a collar. You can fix an address tag or cylinder to it so that the cat can be brought back to you should it become lost while you are away together on holiday. On the way to your holiday destination you can stop, attach a lead to the collar and let the cat stretch its legs without the danger of it running off should something frighten it.

In the first few days, put the collar on for a few minutes each day. Your cat will practically tie itself in knots trying to get rid of it, but if you persevere eventually it will get used to it and not find it strange to wear now and again. Buy a safe collar, one with an elastic part to ensure that your cat will still be able to free itself and not get strangled should the collar get hung up on something. Don't fit it too tightly. You should be able to insert a finger between the collar and your cat's neck.

Once your cat has become used to the collar you can start practising walking it on the lead. In principle, cats can learn this but just how fast and how enjoyable the experience is will depend upon various factors, such as temperament and age. Siamese cats will learn it quickly without too much effort. Older cats will find it more of a problem than younger cats: they are sometimes reluctant if they are not in the right mood.

Apart from collars and leads, pet shops also sell special cat harnesses. These harnesses consist of a collar and a strap that fits around the chest. It's important not to force your cat when trying the harness out for the first time. Put the harness collar and the strap

on the cat. Hold the lead loosely in your hand and walk together with your cat in the direction it chooses. Don't tug on the lead and don't force the cat to walk with you. If everything goes well, reward the cat with a cat treat and then, with the lead in your hand, walk a short distance away from your cat; squat down and try to entice it to come to you. If it comes you can reward with a stroke or by giving it something tasty. Repeat this exercise as long as necessary until you notice that the cat will come to you regardless of where you are standing. This exercise will result in the cat learning to walk with you naturally.

Bullying

No two cats are the same, which is why they behave differently. A relationship between two cats in the same household might be such that it appears that one is bullying the other.

When two cats live together a natural stereotyping develops whereby one cat plays a more dominant roll than the other. This is a remnant of life in the wild. Sometimes it's hardly apparent, if at all, but there are cats that clearly display either dominant or subservient behaviour.

It often occurs that one cat will chase or push another cat off a comfortable spot on a radiator. The dominant cat exercises its right to the best place. What also

A wild cat

happens regularly is that a subservient cat has just had enough time to settle on somebody's lap before the bully comes along and demands the place for itself. Some bullies hide themselves and ambush others of the same sort as they are passing.

Where food is concerned, the dominant cat generally eats before a cat of a lower status but this behaviour is normal amongst wild animals. In fact, in this case it's not bullying in the human sense but an manifestation of dominant and oppressive behaviour.

Remarkable behaviour

As much as cats behave differently for example to dogs, not all cats behave in the same way. They are very much individuals, just like people, which is why it's possible to come across cats with very singular and even striking behaviour and characteristics.

An example of this type of behaviour is a cat that pulls buttons off shirts and blouses or from chair or couch cushions. The behaviour is difficult to explain but some experts believe that it's an excessive form of care and that your cat has an exceptional relationship with you if it acts in this way.

There are also cats that have the unpleasant habit of eating wool. Pure virgin woollens and blankets are chewed into shreds. Other cats

exhibit the same behaviour but show a preference for different materials such as synthetics. Research shows that this type of behaviour only occurs in certain families of cats and may therefore indicate that an inherited factor might be involved.

Some cats become completely entranced if they smell the scent of an olive or a chewed olive stone. They start to act like a female in heat. The scent of catnip can have the same effect on cats too. These sorts of remarkable behaviour, however, are not necessarily inherited. Any cat can start to display them at any time.

Poor hygiene

Some cats have become used to doing the necessary next to the cat litter box instead of in it. Mostly they do this if they think that the cat litter tray isn't clean enough, but the fact is that they are clean animals and they won't just do it anywhere in the house, but always right next to the cat litter box. If your cat has only recently started this type of behaviour it's still correctable as long as you make sure that the litter tray is always clean and smells clean. Some cats have an aversion to strongly smelling cleaning products, so when you clean the litter box with household bleach, let it dry well after on a paper towel.

Cats are very well behaved. They prefer not to foul their surroun-

dings, which is why they bury their faeces, also in cat litter boxes. It's not surprising that a cat will not use a dirty box. There are also fastidious cats, which won't use a litter box even if it's only been used once. In that case, the only solution is to clean the box every time it's used. If you spread a very thin layer of grit in it and always flush it out with hot water once it's been used, you will increase the chances of the cat using it.

Place litter boxes on a surface that is easily cleanable like floor tiles or plastic floor covering so that it's not a disaster if a cat occasionally makes a mistake.

Visiting the vet

A well cared for and well-fed cat has a reduced risk of becoming ill. Nevertheless, you will need to visit a vet from time to time even with a healthy cat, even if it's only to keep it healthy!

Vaccination

Fleas, worms and ticks are tiny parasites, but they are still visible to the naked eye. Cats can also become seriously sick from invisible parasites. That's why having your cat vaccinated is one of the most important measures you can take to keep it healthy. Vaccination can protect cats from a number of serious sicknesses that often have a deadly end.

Feline enteritis

This is justifiably 'the most feared sickness of all time'. It is a highly infectious virus which causes the following symptoms: high fever in excess of 103 °F (39.5 °C), apathy, no appetite, an inflated, 'sticky' coat, vomiting (greenish, foaming slime), diarrhoea and dehydration (the cat wants to

drink but can't). Young cats are particularly susceptible. The sickness develops so quickly that medicines are of little real help: the majority of cases result in death. Because this disease is so infectious, never visit anybody that has a cat suffering from it! It should be clear from the above that every cat needs to be regularly inoculated against Feline Enteritis!

Cat flu

This sickness is just as infectious as feline enteritis but not so deadly. Cats suffering from it can survive to an old age but they will never fully recover. The symptoms can be equally unpleasant for the patient and those in the neighbourhood. Cat flu is a complaint in which a virus causes infection in the mucus membrane of the airways. Cats suffering from it can become very sick. Often they won't eat because they simply can't taste anything. This factor can make recovery difficult.

The first symptoms are runny eyes and a dirty runny nose. It can remain like this for some time before the real sneezing begins. At a later stage the cat can sneeze continuously, spraying long, dirty, yellow strings of mucus around. Other symptoms are: fever, dribbling and sores on the tongue or the eyelids. A vet must be asked to treat any cat showing the initial signs of the illness. Cats often are left with a dripping nose and runny eyes. If your cat is suffering from cat flu avoid all contact with other cat owners. Humans can also spread the disease. An additional danger is that apparently healthy cats can carry the virus and infect other cats without ever showing symptoms themselves.

Vaccination schedule

Whenever your cat goes to an animal hostel or travels outside the country, you need to arrange to have a number of vaccinations carried out well in advance. They don't provide instant protection

Use a special transport basket for your visit to the vet

and in most cases are only valid one month after they have been given. The validity of a rabies vaccination is a maximum one year. If you live in the UK and are planning to take your cat abroad, make sure you abide by the rabies regulations, check with your vet or the RSPCA if necessary.

Sickness symptoms
The following signs indicate that all is not well with your cat: behaviour other than its normal behaviour, reduced appetite, apathy and an inflated coat.
Cats that don't feel physically well raise their coats. They regulate their body temperature in this way when they have a fever. Sick cats will generally not eat. If your cat refuses food for longer than two days, you should take to your vet. Sick cats mostly sit still or curl up in a quiet place.

Pain is also an indication that something is wrong. Cats in pain growl or bite when they are touched. Other symptoms that always need to be taken very seriously are fever, discharge from the nose or eyes, pus-like discharge from the vagina, difficulty with urinating, blood in the urine, cramp, dribbling, a swollen but limp feeling belly and round bald patches in the fur.

Fever is a symptom of serious infectious illness. Discharges from the nose and eyes indicate Cat flu. Difficulty with urinating and/or

ous the worms crawl out of the cats anus and in the most extreme cases the cat may even vomit them. Lint worms consist of a long row of segments with a head at the front. If your cat has lint worm you will find rice like objects in the fur around the cats anus and in its bedding: these are lint worm segments and as long as the head of the lint worm is in the cats body new segments will continue to be formed.

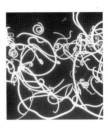

Roundworm

blood in the urine occurs with serious complaints of the urinary tracts. Cramp can occur in weaning kittens and in cats that have been poisoned. Round, bare patches in the fur can be an indication of ringworm (Microsporum), a contagious fungal infection. Peritonitis goes together with a swollen stomach. Always visit your vet as quickly as possible in case of one or more of the above mentioned symptoms should appear. Consult your vet also if one are in doubt about your cat's physical condition at any time, even if there are no visible or concrete symptoms!

Worms

Cats must be free of worms, especially if you have children living at home. You can see from a cats faeces if it has worms. If you can see thin, sometimes moving, spaghetti-like strings about 4 inches (10 cm) long your cat is infected with roundworm. If the infection is seri-

A number of worming preparations are available through your vet or from pet shops. The majority only work on roundworm because these are the most common amongst young cats. Combination preparations are also available that disable a number of types of worms at the same time. Adult cats must be wormed at least twice a year with a preparation that works on all type of worms. Young cats need treatment more regularly. Left untreated over a period of time, worms can cause anaemia.

Fleas

Fleas feed on the cat's blood. They cause not only itching and skin complaints but they can also spread infections such as lint worm. In large numbers they can even lead to anaemia. A cat can also be allergic to the flea's saliva. These allergies can lead to serious skin infections. You can spot fleas because your cat will constantly

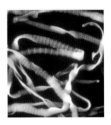

Tapeworm

Flea

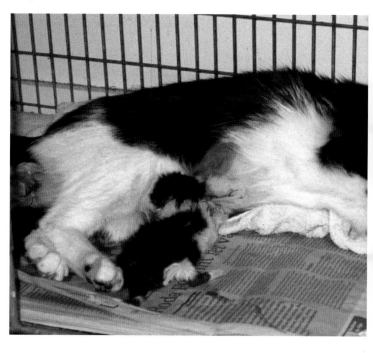

Tick

scratch itself, and concentrations of flea faeces will be evident in the cats fur (small black specs). It's important that fleas are eradicated not just from the cat itself but also from the cats general surroundings. Pesticides for treating animals come in various forms: drops for the back of the neck and in the food, flea collars, long-working sprays and flea powders. The fur of white cats and cats with a white neck can become a little discoloured in the area of a flea collar but the discoloration is harmless. You can keep the cat's immediate surroundings free of fleas by vacuum cleaning them daily. Don't forget the cat's basket, blankets and possibly cushions!

There are a number of sprays available that can be used to treat large areas. Choose a spray that kills both fleas and their larva. A large selection of treatments is available through your vet and from pet shops. Both will be able to provide you with extensive advice on the subject.

Ticks

Ticks are small, spider-like parasites that feed on the blood of their animal or human host. A tick looks like a large blue/grey pea and it can grow to five or ten times its normal size when it has sucked itself full. After a couple of days if detaches itself from the cat.

Cats often become victims in bushes, shrubs, woods or high grass. In addition to causing irritation by sucking blood ticks can transmit diseases. Around the Mediterranean, ticks can cause a serious blood disease. Your vet can prescribe a special medicine for you to take with you if you are taking your cat to southern Europe. This type of disease is luckily not that common in this country although Lyme's disease, which can also infect humans, has been seen. It's very important to prevent ticks so check your cat regularly and fit it with a special anti-tick collar.

Removing a tick must be done very carefully. If you're too abrupt the tick's head can remain in the skin and cause infection. Grasp the tick as close as possible to the skin with a tick remover or another type of tweezers and carefully twist it out. You can also take it in your fingers and twist it out. The wound must be treated with iodine to prevent infection. It's not a good idea to anaesthetise the tick in advance with alcohol or ether. The shock reaction could cause the tick to expel the parasite infected content of its stomach into the cats skin.

Female disorders

There are a couple of disorders that only occur in female cats because they involve the working of the reproductive organs. Uteritis is a common problem.

The cat has a high temperature and behaves very apathetically. There is a discharge from the vagina, often with pus. Take your cat to the vet as soon as you notice these symptoms, so that it can be treated with antibiotics.

Nursing mothers can suffer from infection of the milk glands. The glands are swollen and painful and often take on the appearance of hard, red discs on the stomach. It will be obvious that the female is suffering, and she generally won't continue to feed her kittens. Females with a milk gland infection are often restless and sometimes impossible to handle. Take her to the vet as quickly as possible, because if she really is infected the kittens must not be allowed to drink from her due to the risk of infection to themselves!

Another complaint that appears in nursing females is an acute disruption in calcium levels. The symptoms are convulsions, inability to walk, falling down and leg jerking. These symptoms require urgent medical attention!

Breast tumours regularly occur in older females. These are tumours in the milk glands. If you notice that your female cat has lumps on her stomach you need to have her examined by the vet. Such tumours can be benign but malignant ones also occur. Surgical treatment can be successful if carried out without delay.

Dental problems

A side effect of dental problems is that after a period of time unpleasant odours start to spread from the cat's mouth. This is mostly caused by the presence of tartar. If you open your cat's mouth you can easily see if it has tartar and whether the tartar has caused an infection.

Tartar forms gradually and first becomes obvious when the cat is about eighteen months old. It begins with a few yellow to brown patches on the teeth. The patches are mainly close to the roots of canines and molars, close to the gums. If tartar is not removed in time it forms layers that eventually result in a thick grey mass attached to the teeth that pushes back the gums causing infection. If left untreated tartar will result in the loss of teeth.

Infected gums are scarlet with red edges rather than the usual pink

Dental treatment
of a cat

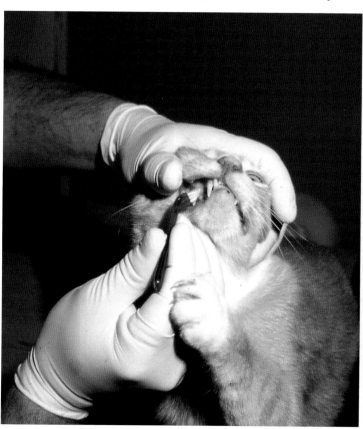

colour. In extreme cases, pus forms. The unpleasant smell starts at a much earlier stage. These problems can be prevented by taking good care of your cat's teeth. Giving it hard dry pet food to eat regularly helps prevent tartar from forming. Cleaning all surfaces of the teeth on a weekly basis helps as well. You can do this with a toothbrush and special toothpaste but you can also use a cloth soaked in a 3% solution of hydrogen peroxide.

If there is a smell coming from your cat's mouth, it's always a good idea to take the cat to the vet. Tartar might need cleaning away, a tooth might need to be removed, or maybe the smell comes from another source such as a kidney disorder for example.

Moulting

Cats normally moult at the end of the summer. Old hair falls out to be replaced by new hair. This process is called moulting. The moult can take several weeks because the coat fall outs very gradually. Females moult after they have been in heat, if they are weaning or have just weaned a litter of kittens. That's why longhaired females often have a thinner shorter coat than males or sterilised females of the same breed.

You need to comb and brush your cat daily when it's moulting. If you don't, you will find hair everywhere, on furniture, carpet and clothing. It's important for both you and your cat that its coat is well maintained: the cats moult will be over quicker, it won't be troubled with tangles and knots and there will be less hair around the house.

There are a number of skin disorders that go hand in hand with dehydration. If you should come across thin or bare patches in your cat's coat, you need to contact your vet without delay. It might be something innocent but some infections, such as ringworm, can also attack humans. This fungal infection can be very difficult to eradicate.

Some cats, primarily castrated males and females, are prone to suffer from hair loss caused by a disruption in their hormonal balance. This sort of complaint needs to be referred to the vet.

The domestic cat's coat is adapted to moderate temperatures. A slightly high temperature combined with dry air in a centrally heated house can cause the cat to lose more hair than normal. Incorrect or insufficient food can also cause problems with a cat's coat. Always give your cat ready-to-eat, complete food. It contains all the important nutrition needed to keep a coat glossy and healthy

Itching

If you should notice that your cat is scratching itself a lot and you are sure that it doesn't have fleas you should take it to the vet as quickly as possible. The chance of recovery is increased if skin complaints are treated at an early stage.

Some cats are allergic to flea saliva. A single fleabite can cause terrible itching. Red spots sometimes appear which the cat scratches open whereby the skin becomes infected and the itching continues. In such circumstances you won't get far without the assistance of a vet and a good flea treatment.

A vet should always be asked to examine red, irritated skin and hair loss. It could be ringworm, a

complaint that can be transferred to humans. Young children are especially at risk. Contrary to the impression given by its name, this is a fungal infection and not caused by a worm.

Some cats suffer from regular itching attacks that cause them to scratch and bite themselves and lose a lot of hair. The most commonly affected are spayed females and castrated males. This stubborn complaint returns regularly and is caused by hormonal imbalance. It's a good idea to consult your vet if you are unsure about the condition of your cat's skin or hair.

Body temperature

The cat's normal body temperature is about 100.5 °F (38 °C) but it's a little higher in the evening than in the morning. It's important that you are able to take your cat's temperature to decide if you need to take it to the vet because an abnormally high temperature can be the first signs of an infectious illness. Your cat has a fever if its temperature is higher than 103 °F (39.5 °C). In this case call the vet immediately.

Some cats are so relaxed that they won't protest at all if you need to take their temperature rectally (via the anus). Others resist so violently that it's impossible to do it without having somebody assist you by restraining the cat. Make sure you have assistance the first time you try it with your cat. Grease a thermometer with a little Vaseline. Lift up the tail with one hand and carefully insert thermometer in the cat's anus with the other hand while your assistant restrains the cat. You can remove and read the

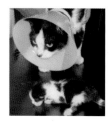

A hood prevents that the cat can bite or scratch at a wound

thermometer after about two minutes. Feverish cats often raise their coats. They appear fluffier than normal and often hide in corners. The so-called third eyelid, in the innermost corner of the eye, partially closes over the eyes. Combined with increased body temperature these are signs of a disorder or sickness.

Runny eyes

As mentioned, runny eyes can be a symptom or a result of cat flu but there can be a less serious cause. It can be a temporary reaction to an injury, for example if an eye has been damaged in a fight with another cat or by a twig. Foreign objects such as a grass seed or a grain of sand will also cause the eyes to water.

In this case the cat will often rub the eye with its paws. Watery eyes often trouble Persian cats. Sometimes their tear ducts are missing but often they are simply blocked so that the only way for the tears to escape is via the eyes. If your cat suffers from runny eyes take it to the vet. Runny eyes need to be cleaned regularly with a cotton bud soaked in tepid water (boiled first).

Urinary problems

If you notice that your cat has problems urinating you should take it to the vet without delay because it may indicate urinary disorders such a bladder infection or feline lower urinary tract disease. These are serious infections that need to be treated without delay.

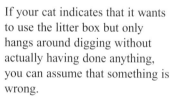

If your cat indicates that it wants to use the litter box but only hangs around digging without actually having done anything, you can assume that something is wrong.
In the majority of cases the cat's behaviour is telling you that the litter is too dirty for its liking. The solution is simply: thoroughly clean the litter box without delay. If this doesn't help it's possible that the cat has a urinary problem.

Although all cats can be troubled by this problem at some time or another, males are more often affected. This is because the male's urethra is smaller than the female's. Feline lower urinary tract disease (crystallised minerals that get stuck in the bladder) can cause an obstruction. The infection that this can cause can seriously endanger your cat's health. Urgent treatment is needed, especially if you notice blood in the urine!

Travel

There are actually few reasons to stop taking your cat on holiday with you. Adventurous trekking holidays to distant countries are hardly suitable, but if you are going to a hotel, bed and breakfast, camping or to an apartment where pets are welcome, your cat can enjoy a vacation too!

Holidays

A cat that's going to travel needs to be in excellent physical condition. If your cat is old or handicapped it's best if you leave it at home. Before you leave one or two things will need to be arranged. For foreign travel in any event you will need to be able to present a recent declaration of health (variable from not older than a month to two days). It also needs to be vaccinated against rabies. You also need to be able to produce a rabies certificate whenever it's requested, issued by the veterinary service. Vaccination against rabies is valid from one month after the date of vaccination. Some countries also have quarantine requirements. Check for details well in advance with your travel agent or your vet.

Don't forget to find out if your cat is welcome at your chosen holiday destination when you are booking a hotel, bed and breakfast or camping site. Always request a written confirmation to avoid an unpleasant surprise on arrival.

It's preferable to take a supply of food with you that your cat is used to. This will prevent possible digestion problems. Your cat will adjust more quickly to abnormal conditions if it has some of its own things with it such as its basket, blanket and toys. You naturally need to take the litter box with you on vacation too. Put it in the bathroom, so that the carpet in the room or apartment doesn't get fouled by accident.

Let your cat get used to its new surroundings for the first few days. The first day you should leave it alone as little as possible, especially if it's the cat's first trip. Keep windows and doors closed and let staff know that there is a cat in your room so that they can take this into account.

Find out the telephone number and address of a local vet for the eventuality that you should need urgent help. It's also handy for your cat to wear a tag showing your holiday address and telephone number just in case your cat gets lost.

Travel Sickness

Cats appear to suffer less from travel sickness than dogs, but this does not mean that cats are particularly fond of travelling. There are a couple of things that you can do to make a long car journey as pleasant as is possible. Make sure that your cat gets used to its travel basket before the journey. If you put it in the room a month before your vacation your cat will have the opportunity to get used to it gradually and maybe sleep in it occasionally.

Stop feeding a couple of hours prior to departure and give the cat

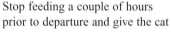

Use a good travel
basket

only a little water. It's a nuisance if a cat 'has to go' when you are already underway and, except in a real emergency, the travelling basket makes it impossible. The cat will only foul the basket in the most extreme circumstances. Don't place the cat in a draught such as by a half-open window, and if it's travelling on your lap, put its collar and lead or harness on. Take regular breaks. They are just as important for you as for your cat. Make sure you have enough bottled drinking water with you. Offer your cat some now and again but don't give it any regular food! Cats meow a lot when they are travelling. It's a sign that they feel insecure.

Animal hostels

Whenever it's impossible to take your cat with you on holiday you can have it looked after at an animal hostel. Most cats adjust there

quite quickly, but there are those who miss their owners so badly that they more or less waste away. They lose their appetite and their condition worsens. If you have such a cat it is better to leave it at home, and have somebody look after it. It will find your absence easier to bear in familiar surroundings.

A cat must be healthy if it's to be accepted by an animal hostel. It also needs to have been vaccinated for Feline Enteritis and cat flu, and it also needs to have been fitted with an identity chip.

Make a reservation well in advance because the majority of animal hostels are completely full in the holiday season especially in and around cities. Ask if you may come to see the facilities, also to discuss any special requirements. Is your cat welcome if it has to take particular medicines or is on

a diet? Can your cats share the same accommodation? You can also ask if your cat can take its own toys and basket although this is not always allowed.

Going by air

Cats can always be transported by air, as airfreight. They travel in their own transport kennel, which is required to conform to certain conditions in terms of weight and dimensions.

The cargo spaces used in aircraft to transport animals are heated and kept under normal atmospheric pressure, so your cat won't feel any discomfort. It's a good idea though to let it get used in advance to being temporarily housed in a transport kennel which is sized precisely to fit the cat. Your cat won't of course be flown free of charge. If you travel in the same aircraft an overweight baggage charge normally applies.

Very occasionally, you might be able to keep your cat with you, but you will need to obtain permission in advance when booking your flight. You can ask the airline concerned how your cat is allowed to travel. In most cases, it won't be possible to carry it on your lap but some will accept it if it's well 'packed' in a small travel basket. A cat carried loose in a cabin can cause a nuisance to other passengers. Some people are allergic; others are frightened of cats or simply hate them. In combination with a fear of flying this can produce all sorts of unpleasant reactions that the cabin staff will want to avoid for safety reasons. That's why strict rules apply to the transport of animals by air.

For air travel, special crates are required

Worth knowing

Electronic identification

A modern and effective way to trace a lost cat is, the chip. This method of identification is above all animal friendly.

A chip, standardised worldwide and the size of a large grain of rice, makes it possible to identify a cat electronically. The vet implants the chip just under the surface of the cat's skin using a syringe. The cat feels no pain and

chip

experiences no side effects. The chip can be read with a chip reader. The reader interrogates the chip and the chip replies with its own code (the transponder number). The code is registered in a database.

The chip's code can't be changed or erased and its life is practically unlimited. This offers clear advantages over other methods of identification. A cat can, for example, lose an identification tag or address holder.

Every year hundreds of lost or stray cats end up in animal hostels. The majority of animal ambulances, animal hostels and police stations are equipped with a reader device. An animal fitted with a chip is nearly always returned to its home.

Toxic garden and house plants

Common mock orange
Laburnum
(the whole plant)
Autumn crocus
(very toxic tubers)
Holly (berries)
Ivy (berries)
Cherry laurel (leaves)
Lathyrus (stems)
Lilly of the valley (the whole plant)
Mistletoe (berries)
Nightshade (the whole plant)

Narcissus (bulbs)
Foxglove
Deadly nightshade (berries)
Cyclamen (tubers)
Dieffenbachia
Brugmansia (the whole plant is highly toxic)
Helleborus (rootstock very toxic)
Oleander (very toxic)
Philodendron
Tulip (bulbs)
Burning bush
Spurge (milky sap)
Caster-oil plant (beans)

Internet and useful addresses

A great deal of information can be found on the internet. Clubs and breed societies can also help with additional information or answer your questions.

A selection of websites with interesting details and links to other sites and pages is listed here. Sometimes pages move to another site or address. You can find more sites by using the available search-machines.

www.cats.org.uk
Cats Protection rescues and re-homes unwanted and abandoned cats, and promotes responsible cat ownership.

www.pedigreecat.co.uk
These pages are dedicated to Pedigree Cats in the UK. The site contains photographs and information about the different breeds of cats that are currently available in Great Britain. There are also links to cat breeders, registering organizations and other cat related sites.

www.catworld.co.uk
An informative site where you can find more on breeds, book reviews, health, show news, ask experts and much more.

www.fabcats.org
A charity which promotes the health and welfare of cats by making the latest information available to vets, cat breeders and owners.

www.cats-dogs.co.uk
Provides a quick route to finding the services you require for your cats. Finds catteries, boarding kennels, veterinary surgeons or other pet services & supplies.

www.cats-inverurie.co.uk
Rescues and re-homes cats in the North East of Scotland.

www.catsnkittens.co.uk
This site is full of information on Britain's most popular pet. Breeders, advice, kittens for sale, studs, clubs & societies, boarding catteries, shows and much more!

www.petplanet.co.uk
Find information on dogs, cats and pets here. You'll find breed profiles of dogs and cats or your nearest vets, kennels, catteries or breeds societies. Visit Pet Talk and ask for advice about specific breeds, or share stories about dogs and cats with our thousands of regular visiting pet lovers.

Usefull adresses

The Governing Council of the Cat Fancy Great Britain Governing Council of the Cat Fancy or GCCF
4 - 6 Penel Orlieu
Bridgwater, Somerset
TA6 3PG, UK
Tel: +44 (0)1278 427575
Website: http://ourworld.compu-serve.com/homepages/GCCF_CATS/index.htm
email: info@gccfcats.org

Cat clubs
A Directory of Cat Clubs and Societies
This directory lists some of the many breed societies, area cat clubs in the British Isles.
http://members.aol.com/cattrust/catclubs.htm#S

Cat club Northern Ireland
Catclub.net
8 Deramore Gardens
Belfast , N. Ireland
BT7 3FN
Tel: (028) 90597251
e-mail: charlotte@catclub.net
http://www.catclub.net/home.cfm

Other books from About Pets

- The Border Collie
- The Boxer
- The Cavalier King Charles Spaniel
- The Cocker Spaniel
- The Dalmatian
- The Dobermann
- The German Shepherd
- The Golden Retriever
- The Jack Russell Terrier
- The Labrador Retriever
- The Puppy
- The Rottweiler
- The Canary
- The Budgerigar
- The Cockatiel
- The Lovebird
- The Parrot
- The Kitten
- The Dwarf Hamster
- The Dwarf Rabbit
- The Ferret
- The Gerbil
- The Guinea Pig
- The Hamster
- The Mouse
- The Rabbit
- The Rat
- The Goldfish
- The Tropical Fish
- The Snake

Key features of the series are:
- Most affordable books
- Packed with hands-on information
- Well written by experts
- Easy to understand language
- Full colour original photography
- 70 to 110 photos
- All one needs to know to care well for their pet
- Trusted authors, veterinary consultants, breed and species expert authorities
- Appropriate for first time pet owners
- Interesting detailed information for pet professionals
- Title range includes books for advanced pet owners and breeders
- Includes useful addresses, veterinary data, breed standards.

about pets

Cat tips

- A cat is in its element out of doors but must not lose its bond with its home.
- Give your cat only complete, ready-to-eat food.
- Eating together can be stimulating but it can also be distracting.
- Skin disorders in cats can be infectious and difficult to cure
- The dominant cat controls the best places.
- If you are often away from home your cat will benefit from having a playmate.
- Cats will sometimes have nothing to do with strangers.
- Don't breed a litter until you have found a good home for the kittens.
- Get your male castrated in time to prevent spraying

- Don't exterminate only the fleas, the larva need treating as well.
- Electronic identification is an effective method of reuniting a lost cat with its owner.
- Poor cat hygiene can have a wide variety of causes.
- A longhaired cat needs intensive care.
- A cat that never goes outside will definitely need a scratching post.
- Keep your cat inside as much as possible when fledglings are leaving their nests.
- Children can be very loving but not always very gentle with cats.